First Lessons
in Ballet

First Lessons in Ballet

by Lise Friedman

with photographs by K. C. Bailey
Suki Schorer, consultant

WORKMAN PUBLISHING · NEW YORK

All photographs copyright © K. C. Bailey.

Library of Congress Cataloging-in-Publication
Data

Friedman, Lise.
First lessons in ballet / by Lise Friedman; with
photographs by K.C. Bailey.
p. cm.
Summary: Photographs, captions, callouts, and
text provide an interactive introduction to ballet,
covering stretching, the five basic positions, and
more complicated moves.
ISBN 0-7611-1804-7 (hc)
ISBN 0-7611-1352-5 (pbk)
1. Ballet dancing Juvenile literature. [1. Ballet
dancing.] I. Title.
GV1787.5.F75 1999
792.8—dc21   99-27272
CIP

Workman books are available at special discounts
when purchased in bulk for premiums and sales
promotions as well as for fund-raising or educa-
tional use. Special editions can also be created to
specification. For details, contact the Special
Sales Director at the address below.

Workman Publishing Company, Inc.
708 Broadway
New York, NY 10003-9555
www.workmanweb.com

Printed in Hong Kong

First printing October 1999
10 9 8 7 6 5 4 3 2 1

Like a dance class, *First Lessons in Ballet* is the result of many people working closely together. My thanks to all of them.

To the dancers who posed, leaped, and spun with boundless energy: Pamela Alviar, Yamise Cameron, Alina Dronova, Zalman Grinberg, Christina Hernandez, Ezra Hurwitz, Rebecca Krohn, Anna McLean, Chita O'Keeffe, Nickolas Porrello, Nersy Rodriguez, Gabrielle Salvatto, and Eric Underwood.

To the dedicated teachers who provided access and support: project consultant Suki Schorer, for her pedagogic expertise and buoyant energy, and Olga Kostritzky, School of American Ballet; Diana Byer, New York Theatre Ballet School; Maggie Christ and

Lynn Muller, Ballet Tech; Tina Ramirez, Ballet Hispanico School of Dance.

To photographer K. C. Bailey, for her unerring way with line, form, and the serendipitous moment; costume designer Kathlene Mobley, for her inspired way with lycra, tulle, and tiaras; and Abizaid Arts, for the use of their studios.

To Peter Workman, for his enthusiasm; Sally Kovalchick, for her guidance; Anne Kostick and Kathleen King,

for their insight and acumen; and Elizabeth Johnsboen, for her constructive eye.

To the vendors who donated goods and services: Capezio Ballet Makers, Danskin, Inc., Gourmet Garage, Musical Score Distributors, and York Construction.

And finally, thanks to my agent, Beth Vesel, for her friendship and perseverance, and to my family, for urging me on.

introduction

Ballet is a great way to express your feelings, strengthen your body, and improve your sense of grace. And it's also a lot of fun. As you wander through this book, you'll notice that many of the terms are in French. Why? Because ballet, although it began in Italy, owes its popularity to King Louis XIV of France. King Louis was so crazy about ballet that he took lessons every day, started the first ballet academy, and ordered his teacher, Pierre Beauchamps, to write down all the steps. Soon ballet had its own language and specially trained dancers. That is why the names of the exercises and positions are in French—why we still say *grand-plié* when we're talking about a deep knee bend.

Studying ballet is not like going to school: as long as you keep dancing, you never grad-uate! Every dancer, from beginner to prima ballerina, "takes class," and every class, from the first level to profes-sional, begins and ends the same way: you start with exer-cises at the barre, move into the center of the studio for slow and fast movements, and finish with big jumps across the floor. The students who helped make this book lead you through a ballet class, starting with first position.

Rebecca, who has been danc-ing for twelve years, has per-fected many of the moves, while the kids are just learning to dance. They show you all sorts of stretches, the basic positions, and steps. If you're interested in studying ballet or are already taking class, *First Lessons in Ballet* will give you a preview of what's to come. You may well be the next prima ballerina or premier danseur. *Voilà!*

THE STUDIO

The studio is a big open room with plenty of space to dance. The surface of the floor is covered with either smooth wood or vinyl. And it should be put together in a special way—the supports laid down in a woven pattern, like a basket—so that it has a little "bounce" or "give." This

enables you to jump higher and land softer, and it feels better on your joints than a floor that has no "give."

THE BARRE

When you look around the studio, you'll probably see wooden or metal *barres* (horizontal bars) attached to the walls for you to hold while you do your exercises, a big mirror for checking your positions, and maybe a box of rosin on the floor in a corner. *Rosin,* crunchy yellow crystals made from crystallized tree sap, keeps your feet from slipping when you turn and jump. In

addition there may be a piano, or your teacher will play selections from tapes or CDs. It's important to move in time to the music.

CLOTHING

In the same way everything in the studio has a special purpose, your dance clothes are designed with movement in mind. Most dance clothes are made of stretchy materials

getting started

that allow you to move freely and efficiently. Clothes should fit very close to the body so that your teacher can see if you are using your muscles properly. Boys usually wear a white T-shirt and black tights, while girls wear leotards over light-colored tights, sometimes adding a short dance skirt. Certain schools require special colors for each level.

Both boys and girls wear soft shoes called slippers that fit snugly and are made of canvas, leather, or satin. They should be a bit tight when they're brand new because they will stretch. If you wear a small size, your slippers will probably come with elastics sewn in place. With larger

sizes, the elastics come separately, so you'll need to sew them on at home. The elastics should stretch firmly across your insteps and be attached just in front of your ankle bones. Fold the heel forward; the sides crease exactly where your elastics should be sewn. Once you get your slippers on, adjust and tie the drawstring that runs through the top of each one and then tuck in

the loose ends. It's important to be neat.

Girls' hair should be pulled back from the face, and if it's long, tied up securely. Boys don't need to do anything special with their hair, as long as they too can see what they're doing.

Now you have your dance "uniform"!

*Try not
to bounce.*

*Keep
breathing!*

Big Stretches

Before you start your centerwork, try some of these bigger stretches. Even if your muscles feel as stretchy as taffy, remember, you still need to move with care. You should not feel any pain, so go only as far as you feel comfortable. Try to relax into the stretch and hold it for a while.

For big muscle stretches, such as splits, you need to be as warm as possible, so they're done after the barre or at the end of class. Move slowly and carefully during warm-up. It takes time to develop flexibility and strength.

warm-up

WARM-UP

You warm up with gentle stretching and strengthening exercises that prepare your body for dancing. Warm-up is part of your routine, usually done at the very beginning of class, on the floor and at the barre, sometimes with a partner. Stretches help loosen and lengthen your muscles so that you can move with ease and flexibility, while exercises like sit-ups and push-ups strengthen your muscles.

first position

The five basic positions of the legs and arms are the building blocks for ballet. The better you know the basic positions the more secure you'll feel moving from one position or step to the next. First practice the positions of the feet at the barre, then try them in the center of the room with the corresponding arm positions. These are safe to try on your own.

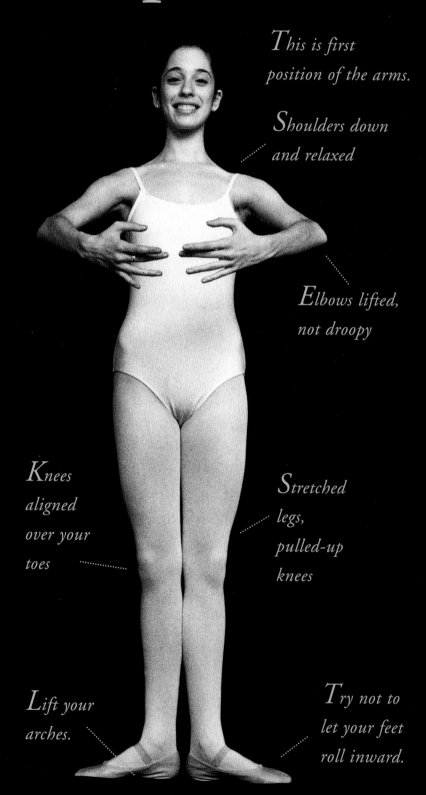

This is first position of the arms.

Shoulders down and relaxed

Elbows lifted, not droopy

Knees aligned over your toes

Stretched legs, pulled-up knees

Lift your arches.

Try not to let your feet roll inward.

première

First position, or *première* (prehm-YAHR), is quiet and contained. Put your heels together and toes apart so that your feet form a wide V-shape. Keep your legs nicely stretched and rotated out. This is called turnout; it is a part of every position and movement in ballet. Be sure your feet are not rolled in and your knees are over your toes. Hold your arms in a soft circle in front of your torso, between your chest and navel. (Pretend you're holding a gigantic beach ball.) Let your hands fall into a natural position, then shape them so that your fingers follow the line of your arms. Now imagine that a string is attached to the top of your head, gently pulling up, lengthening your neck and back. See, you're taller already!

Get to know first position. You'll use it again and again in class.

second position

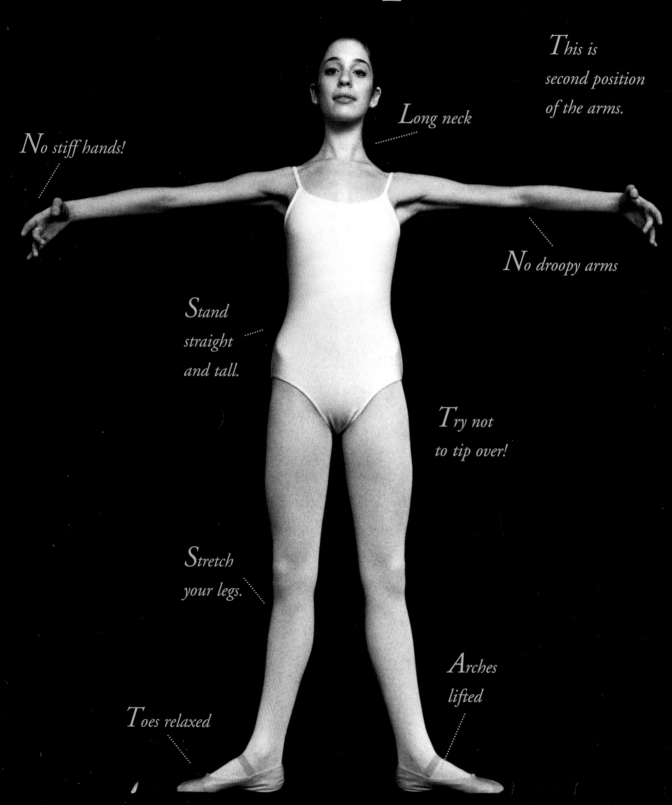

This is
second position
of the arms.

Long neck

No stiff hands!

No droopy arms

Stand
straight
and tall.

Try not
to tip over!

Stretch
your legs.

Arches
lifted

Toes relaxed

seconde

Turnout

Your teacher will remind you to work on your *turnout*. Why? Because it's important in every position and movement in ballet. In correct turnout, your entire leg is turned out to the side, not just your foot. Your turnout should start in your hips. Start rotating your leg outward at the hip joint, and continue down the leg and through the foot, gently turning the muscles out and away from the front. You want to feel both thighs rotating out from the center of your body. Your knees should face the same direction as your toes. Never ever turn out *just* your feet, as you will twist your knees. When your turnout is done properly, it gives your hip joints lots of flexibility and makes it possible to travel sideways without turning away from your audience, which would be very rude.

This is second position, or *seconde* (seh-GOHND). Stand with your feet apart. The distance between your heels should be about the length of one of your feet. Turn out your legs and feet from the tops of your thighs. Stretch your arms out to your sides. Your arms should be slightly rounded, making a curved line, and held just a bit in front of your torso, so that you can see your fingertips out of the corners of your eyes when you look forward. Your hands and fingers stretch softly, extending the line of your arms.

third position

Stretch your hands and fingers softly.

Shoulders relaxed and down

Straight, long back

This is third position of the arms.

Stretched legs

Arches lifted!

Try not to let your feet roll inward.

troisième

Placement

The secret to moving efficiently and easily is proper *placement*, also known as posture or alignment. Proper placement is as important as executing steps, and without it, steps are harder to do and don't look right. Practice in first position. Standing nice and tall, think of your body's center as a line that runs up your spine, through the top of your head, and up to the ceiling. Your weight should be balanced over both feet and your legs turned out from your hip joints. As you lengthen your neck and back, lift your chest slightly and allow your arms to curve a bit at your sides. (Imagine that you have a small grapefruit tucked into each armpit.) You don't need to be practicing ballet steps to practice placement. You can work on it just about any time. Do it while you're brushing your teeth or waiting in line. Eventually, it will become second nature.

In third position, *troisième* (trwah-ZYEM), cross your front heel about halfway in front of your other foot. Try to keep every part of your legs, from the tops of your thighs down through your feet, turning out. This position is done both to the right and to the left. If your right foot is in front, raise your left arm overhead in a semicircle, holding it just slightly forward of your head. Extend your right arm out to your side. If your left foot is in front, then the right arm curves overhead and the left arm reaches out to your side. Beginning dancers often use third position of the feet instead of fifth, which requires more strength.

fourth position

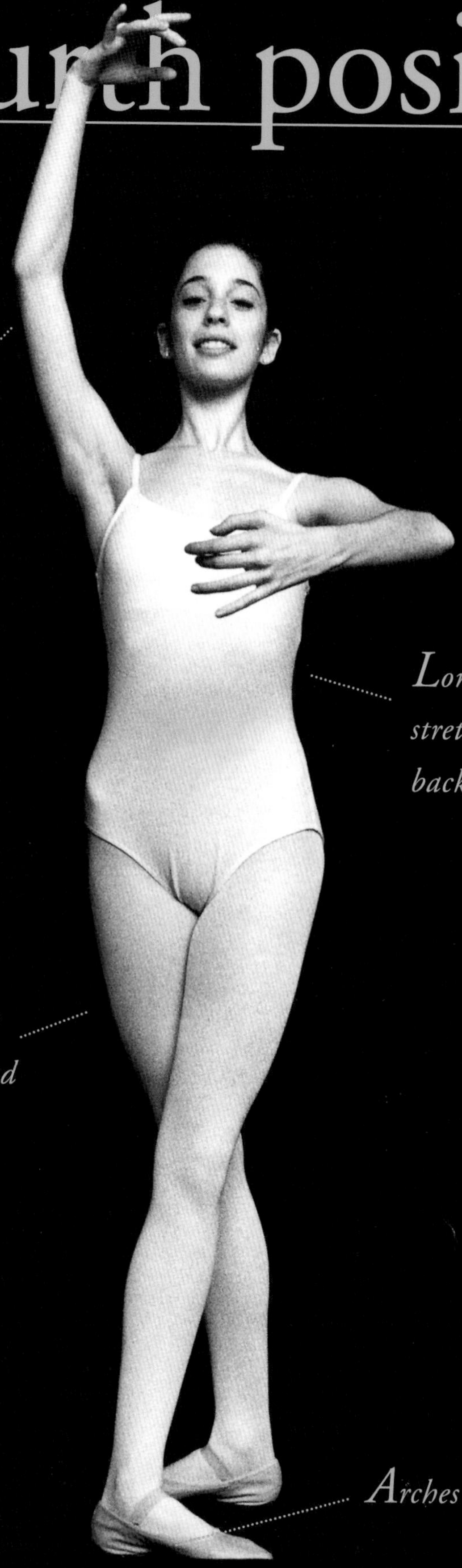

*Arms
gently
curved*

*This is
fourth position
of the arms.*

*Long,
stretched
back*

*Keep your
legs strongly
stretched and
rotated out.*

Arches lifted!

quatrième

In fourth position, or *qua-trième* (kah-tree-EHM), you need to hold onto your turnout. In a crossed fourth position, you place one foot in front of the other, with the forward heel directly in front of the toe of the other foot. In an open fourth position, you place the forward heel in front of the instep of the other foot. In both cases, the space between your feet should be about the length of one of your feet. This position is also done both to the right and to the left. If your right foot is forward, raise your left arm overhead in a semicircle and curve your right arm in front of your body. Do the opposite when your left foot is forward. Keep your torso long and *square to your front,* which means don't twist your body. Pretend you have a headlight on each hip.

Fourth is a difficult position, so take extra time and care.

fifth position

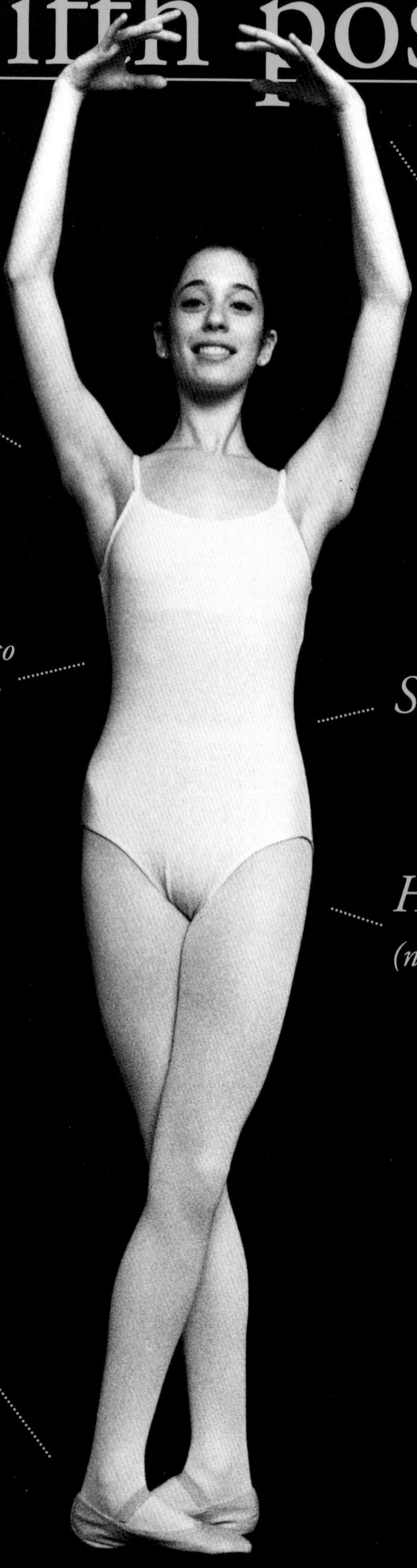

Keep fingers
shaped
and long.

Shoulders
down and
relaxed

This is
fifth position
of the arms.

Torso
lifted

Stomach in

Hips pulled up
(no swaybacks)

Try not to turn
out your feet
beyond the line
of your knees.

cinquième

In fifth position, or *cinquième* (san-KYEM), think of your body as a tall column, reaching for the sky. Turning out from your hip joints and lifting up through your knees and ankles, cross your right foot in front of your left foot, placing your right heel directly in front of your left toes. This position requires flexibility and strength. Lift both arms overhead in a soft circle shape. Hold your arms just forward of your head. Try fifth position with your right foot crossed in front and then with your left foot. Never force yourself into position. It will start to feel natural after a while.

Your arms are as important as your legs in ballet. The many shapes you learn to make with them are called *port-de-bras* (pohr-dih-BRAH), which means "carriage of the arms" in French. The arms complement, extend, and complete the movement and flowing line of the body. The arms help you balance. Think of yourself as a tightrope walker with a balancing pole. If you've ever tried dancing without allowing your arms to move, you know it's hard to move, because your upper body and arms cannot respond to the step. Sometimes your arms and hands tell stories of their own. For example, in certain story ballets arm gestures portray a character or can mean love, fear, or death.

21

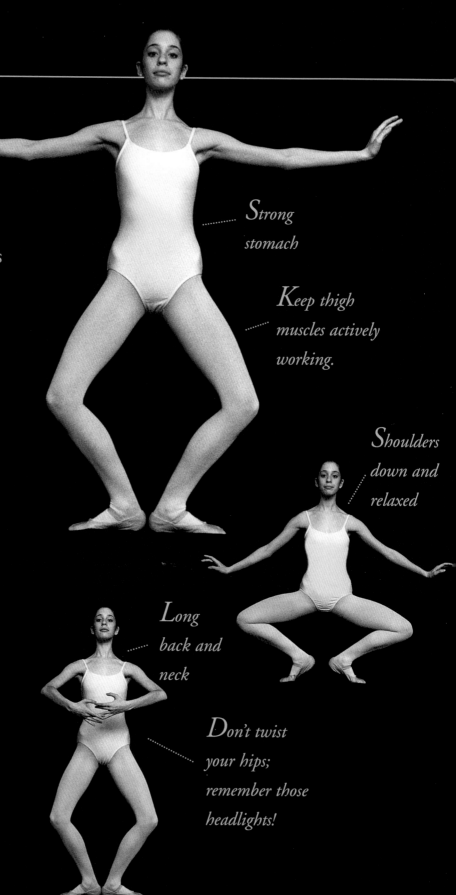

The exercises you do at the barre develop your skills in basic ballet movements and prepare you for centerwork, turning, and big traveling steps you'll learn later on in class. The barre exercises warm up your muscles and give you a chance to work on your turnout and placement. You do each exercise to the right and to the left so that you don't end up lopsided.

Strong stomach

Keep thigh muscles actively working.

Shoulders down and relaxed

Long back and neck

Don't twist your hips; remember those headlights!

pliés

B arre work almost always begins with the *plié* (plee-AY), a basic bending and stretching of the knees. Begin with *demi-plié* (dih-MEE plee-AY), which means "half-plié." Bend your knees only as far as your ankles allow without lifting your heels off the floor. From there, slowly straighten your knees, lengthening through your torso, neck, and head. To do a *grand-plié* (grahn plee-AY), or "large plié," first do a demi-plié, then continue bending your knees, allowing your heels to lift only as far as necessary until your thighs are almost parallel to the floor. As you lower yourself, lift your stomach so that you don't

Your arms are alive, too. As you plié, lower your arms from second position through low fifth position. As you rise, lift your arms through first position, opening them out to second position as you straighten your knees. Keep your movement smooth and continuous.

squat or sit! As you rise, lower your heels as soon as possible. Throughout, try to keep your hips from twisting every which way. Try grand-plié in first, second, and third positions,

and then, do everything all over again on the opposite side. (In second-position grand-plié, your heels never leave the floor.)

23

Don't
clench your
fingers.

Keep your
hips level.

Try not
to clench
your toes.

tendu

Like pliés, *tendu* (tahn-DYU) exercises are done early in class. Their purpose is to train your feet to point: tendu means "stretched." Standing in first position, slide your working foot out to the side, keeping your heel forward and lifting it off the floor as you stretch your foot and point your toes. To close, reverse the movement, pulling your toes back and keeping your heel forward as you move your foot toward first position. Try the same movement to the

Don't grip the barre too hard.

front and back. When you close from a tendu to the back, be extra careful to keep your heel moving forward. Throughout the exercise, your supporting leg stays long, strong, and turned out, and your hips, upper body, and head stay still. Pretend that your foot is a whisk broom softly sweeping the floor as you move your leg in and out.

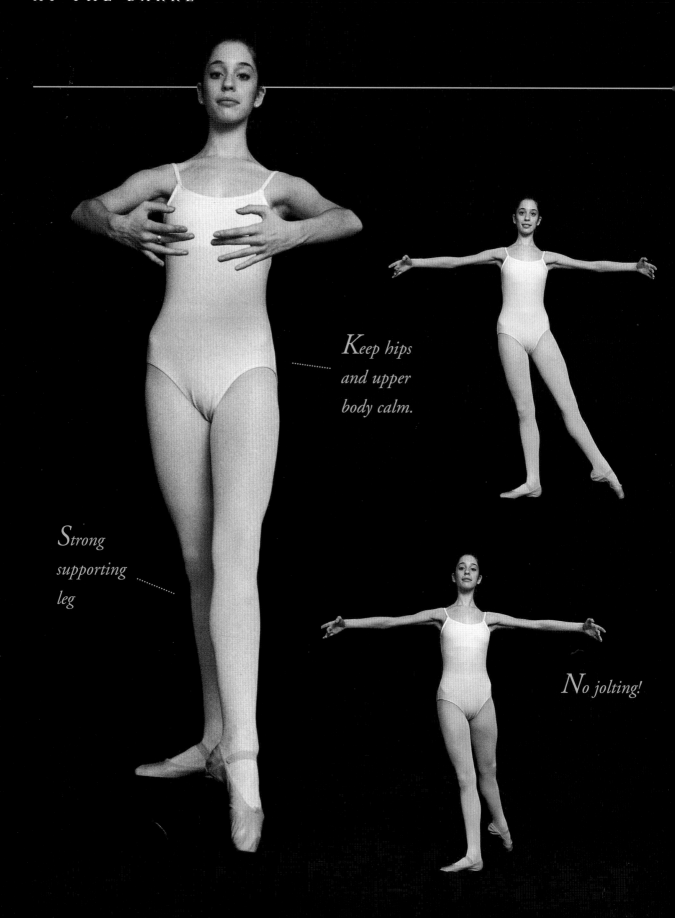

*Keep hips
and upper
body calm.*

*Strong
supporting
leg*

No jolting!

rond de jambe

R*ond de jambe* (rohn dih ZHAHNB) means "circle of the leg." In this exercise, your working foot draws a half-circle to the side of your supporting leg. Here the dancers are doing it *à terre* (ah TAYR), meaning "on the ground." It can also be done *en l'air* (ah LAYR), or "in the air." Starting from first position, brush your foot forward to tendu front. Then move your leg from the front to the side and then around to the back before closing again in first position. Your toes never leave the floor. The trick is to move smoothly from one position to the next without jolting. When you are more advanced you will be able to make the circle without any pauses or stops. Now try the same movement in reverse, circling from tendu back, to the side, the front, and finally closing again in first.

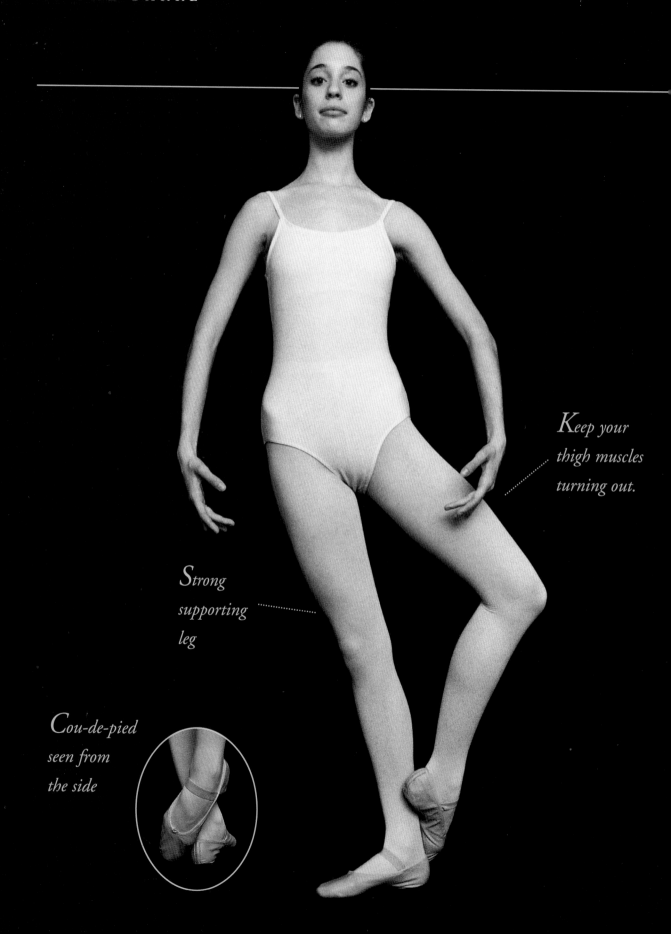

Keep your thigh muscles turning out.

Strong supporting leg

Cou-de-pied seen from the side

cou-de-pied

Cou-de-pied (koo-dih-pee-CAY) means "neck of the foot." (You know this part as your ankle.) This exercise helps develop your feet and strengthen your turnout, and it is a building block for lots of steps that begin by *lifting*, not brushing, your foot off the floor. Cou-de-pied can be done quickly, slowly, smoothly, or powerfully. During the exercise your working foot is very active. It wraps around the part of your leg that's between the top of your ankle bone and the bottom of your calf muscle. In cou-de-pied front, your working heel is in front of the supporting leg's ankle and your toes reach around behind. Try to keep your working knee pulled back and your working foot stretched as it wraps and curves around your "cou" just like a snake curls around a tree trunk. As your foot moves into cou-de-pied imagine that your foot is a snake.

29

Long torso

Hips
square

Supporting
leg stretched
and pulled up

retiré, or passé

Retiré (reh-tee-RAY), or passé (pah-SAY), comes up again and again in ballet and is a good preparation for turning. Starting in fifth position, draw an imaginary line with your front foot (your pointed toes are the pencil) that starts in front of your supporting ankle and travels up the middle of your leg until it reaches the notch right below your knee. Stretch your arms out to your sides as though you are about to fly. If you're feeling really brave—and your teacher says "Go for it!"—try to rise up on your supporting leg to half-toe, relevé.

You might try retiré with your arms in first position.

Long neck

Strong back and stomach

Keep hips square.

Turned out and pointed foot

Straight, stretched legs

grand battement

G *rand battement* (grahn baht-MAHN) is a gigantic and powerful kick done with a straight, turned-out leg. It is usually practiced near the end of the barre work, when your muscles are very warm. First try it slowly to understand the

action of your working leg. Often teachers break the movement into sections, like this: tendu front, then raise

your leg as high as you can without lifting or twisting your hips. Keep both legs stretched and your back long. (Check your turnout. Could you balance a teacup on your raised heel?) Now lower your leg, pausing in tendu before you close. Try this to the side and to the back. Try the same exercise much more rapidly, still stopping in tendu, but throwing the leg into the air. As you become stronger, you will be able to do a grand battement directly from fifth position without pausing in tendu. Use the floor to help you throw the leg high up. When you do grand battement to the back, one leg is stretched long and high behind you, just like an arabesque!

Once your teacher says you're ready to try some exercises away from the barre, center-work is the next step. You begin to truly understand how your body moves in space when you dance away from the barre, in the center of the studio. In this section, you'll work on balance and coordination, as well as some early turning and traveling steps.

1. Croisé devant *(krwah-ZAY dih-VAHN)*, crossed in front
2. A la quatrième devant *(kah-tree-EHM dih-VAHN)*, in fourth front
3. Effacé devant *(ay-fah-SAY dih-VAHN)*, open to the front
4. Ecarté devant *(ay-kahr-TAY dih-VAHN)*, separated, or thrown apart, to the front
5. A la seconde *(sih-GOHND)*, in second
6. Ecarté derrière *(ah-kahr-TAY deh-ree-AYR)*, separated, or thrown apart, behind

7. Effacé derrière *(ay-fah-SAY deh-ree-AYR)*, open to the back
8. A la quatrième derrière *(kah-tree-EHM deh-ree-AYR)*, in fourth behind
9. Croisé derrière *(krwah-ZAY deh-ree-AYR)*, crossed behind
10. Croisé derrière *(krwah-ZAY deh-ree-AYR)*, crossed behind, raised arm opposite working leg.

directions of the body

These positions were created to show off the shapes your body makes in space. Imagine eight lines running along the floor, starting from where you're standing and stretching to each corner, and to the sides and front and back of the room. Each pose is designed to fit on one of these lines.

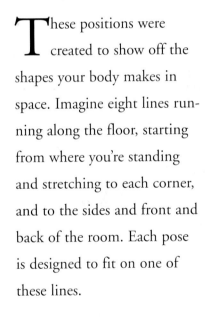

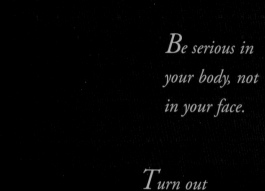

*B*e serious in
your body, not
in your face.

*H*old your
head high.

*K*eep
breathing!

*T*urn out
from your hips.

*L*ift!

*K*eep your
torso square
to your front.

*S*tretch!

*W*ork
your stomach
muscles.

arabesque

Arabesque (ah-rah-BESK) is a balance on one leg with the other stretched long and high behind you. You need lots of strength in your legs, hips, and back, and you use a variety of arm positions. Notice the shape as you lift your torso up and forward a bit to allow your working leg to reach high and continue the curve of your back. Reach one arm forward and the other diagonally back. The arms should complement the line of the working leg. Arabesque is often performed as part of an *adage* (ah-DAHZH), or combi- nation of slow, silky move- ments. It can also be done quickly, with a springing or jumping action. These dancers are in first arabesque.

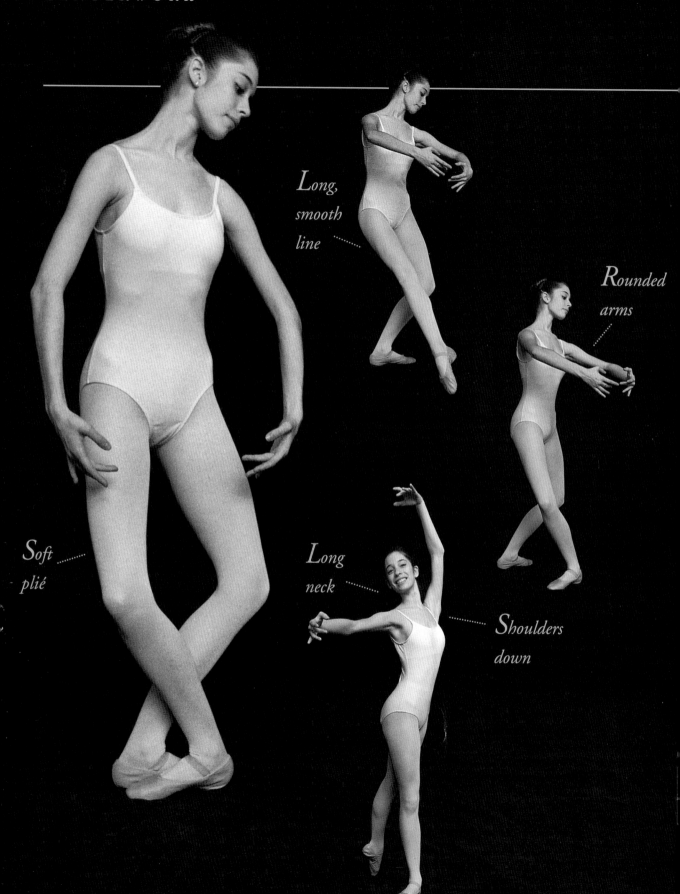

*Long,
smooth
line*

*Rounded
arms*

*Soft
plié*

*Long
neck*

*Shoulders
down*

temps lié

Many positions in ballet are joined by connecting movements, or transitions. Transition movements are just as important as the positions themselves. Both involve a transfer of weight. *Temps lié* (tahn lee-AY), which means "time bound together," is one of the most common. It allows you to flow from one shape to another. Think of temps lié as a little dance that can move in many directions and at different speeds (*tempi*). Here, the dancers are moving forward in space, or *en avant*.

Facing a front corner of the room, start in fifth position croisé, with your arms in second position. Move into demi-plié, and bring your arms into low fifth position, inclining your head away from the mirror. While in plié, slide your front foot forward, lift your arms into first position.

Then, start to transfer your weight smoothly through demi-plié in fourth position. (Feel both feet firmly on the floor.) Continue transferring all your weight onto your front foot, finishing with your back foot extended in tendu croisé derrière. At the same time, lift your arms into third position as your head moves into the croisé derrière line.

Step lively!

One foot replaces the other.

Long back

Stretch those legs.

pas de bourrée

Pas de bourrée (pah dih boo-RAY) is another common transition movement. (A bourrée is an old French dance.) Pas de bourrée is a useful traveling step and can be done rapidly or slowly. Think of your foot action as the plucking of violin strings, delicate and precise. The exercise often begins and ends the same way, in demi-plié, with your working foot in coupé derrière. (*Coupé* means "cut." Your beautifully pointed foot springs quickly and sharply into position just in back of your ankle, a little higher than the ankle bone but not as high as retiré.)

From the starting position, step on demi-pointe (half-toe) onto your back foot. At the same time, extend your front leg in a low side position, or à la seconde. Step onto the extended leg, forming a small

second position. Now lift your other leg into a low second before you transfer your weight back onto that leg. You finish the exercise the same way you begin it, but now you're on the opposite foot. Pas de bourrée is done on both sides. Rebecca has tried this move with her working foot

lifting high into retiré.

41

Keep breathing.

port-de-bras

en grand quatrième

P*ort-de-bras en grand quatrième* (por-dih-BRAH ahn grahn kah-tree-EHM), which means "carriage of the arms in a large fourth position," is a great stretch for your legs and back and a chance for you to be expressive with your arms. Step forward into a large fourth position lunge. Plié deeply on your front leg, keeping your back leg long and stretched. As you take your torso forward, your back and neck lengthen. Concentrate on the shapes your arms are making as you move them through the positions: from second, through first, and up into fifth position. They should feel smooth as molasses. As you rise, imagine you're waking up in a beautiful flower garden after a long, restful sleep.

*K*eep your
legs stretched.

*S*trong
ankles—
try not to
wobble!

relevé

The word *relevé* (reh-lih-VAY) means "lifted or raised." Relevés make your feet and legs stronger and help prepare you for jumping and turning. Relevé action is similar to a plant's stem that grows up toward the sun while its roots reach down to the earth. Think of the top of your head as a young plant's shoot and your feet as its roots. Stand in first position, facing the barre. Keep your weight over the balls of your feet so that you have a nice strong base. Now, holding the barre as lightly as you can, with your legs stretched, press down through the floor and lift up through the top of your head as your heels lift slowly and smoothly. Everything stays straight as you rise up, until you're on demi-pointe, or half-toe. What goes up must come down, of course. But you don't want to crash. Lower your heels slowly and smoothly, keeping your weight over the balls of your feet and holding on to your turnout. Come down softly until your entire foot is on the floor. Once you've mastered relevé at the barre, you can practice it in the center.

All the exercises you have done so far have prepared your body for jumping. You must begin every jump with a strong demi-plié. On your landing, your toes touch the floor first, then gently lower through your foot as you make a demi-plié. Always land with your knees facing the same direction as your toes.

Hold on to your turnout.

Press your entire foot into the floor as you push off.

Stretch your legs and feet as you go up.

Soft landing, like a cat

changement

Changement (shahnj-MAHN), which means changing, can be a small, quick step. First, demi-plié in fifth position, and push through your feet so that you spring off the floor as your knees stretch and your feet point in the air. While you're in the air, change your feet, passing through a small first position, and land with the opposite foot forward. Keep your energy focused upward. After you've mastered change-ment, your teacher might ask you to do the exercise with *épaulement* (ah-pohl-MAHN), or placement of the shoulders. Épaulement adds a lovely line to many steps. Start in fifth position croisé, right foot front. As you jump, shift your body to the *en face* (ahn fahs), or facing position, to land in fifth position croisé.

Try
not to
kick.

No
thuds!

Stretch
your legs
and feet.

sissonne

Sissonne (see-sohn) is an energetic jump from both feet that can travel forward, sideways, backward, and on a diagonal. It can be done quickly or slowly, high or low. Advanced dancers can even do sissonne with beats (the legs scissor together in the air). Here, the dancers are moving forward on the diagonal. That is, their bodies are facing a front corner of the studio.

Starting from demi-plié in fifth position, push off on a forward diagonal, immediately stretching both legs. Your front leg moves rapidly forward as your back leg lifts to first arabesque. Your arms, which complement your legs, are in first arabesque, too. Look out over your forward arm in the direction of your jump. As you land on your front leg quickly bring the working leg down through tendu and close again in fifth position demi-plié.

Be sure to hold up your torso and back with strength so that your body doesn't heave back and then fall forward. Because sissonne is a difficult step, your teacher might have you stretch your legs and pause between jumps.

*Keep your
hips and back
in one piece.*

*Remember
to spot.*

*Bring your
hips and back
over your
front leg.*

*No wiggling
in your torso*

About Direction

If a turn moves toward your
supporting leg, it's called
en dedans (ahn dih-DAHN), or
inward. If it moves away, it's
called *en dehors* (ahn dih-AWR),
or outward.

*Always turn in
the direction of
your front foot.*

piqué turns

*P*iqué (pee-KAY) turns travel across the floor and can be done in a straight line or in a circle. Piqué means "speared or pricked." Before you start spinning, practice stepping onto half-toe with a straight, strong supporting leg. From demi-plié in fifth position, take a big step to your side, opening your arms into second position. As you step onto demi-pointe, pick your other foot up into a high coupé back and close your arms to a rounded first position. Try to balance for a moment before closing your working leg to the back in fifth position plié. Extend your front leg to your side for the next piqué. When your teacher feels you're ready, you can add a turn as you step into piqué.

Learning to Spot

*W*ith all the whirling in ballet, how do dancers keep from getting dizzy? They learn how to "spot." Stand still and look straight ahead. Find a place or an object or a mark on the wall at approximately eye level to look at, and slowly turn your body, keeping your eyes on that spot as long as you can. (If you're looking in the mirror, you can focus on your eyes.) When you can't turn your body anymore without moving your head (you're not an owl, after all!), quickly whip your head around and find your spot again as you continue your turn. First your body starts turning, then your head snaps around to the front, and finally your body continues turning around until facing front. Try this several times to your right and then to your left. Take a break—especially if the room starts to whirl!

51

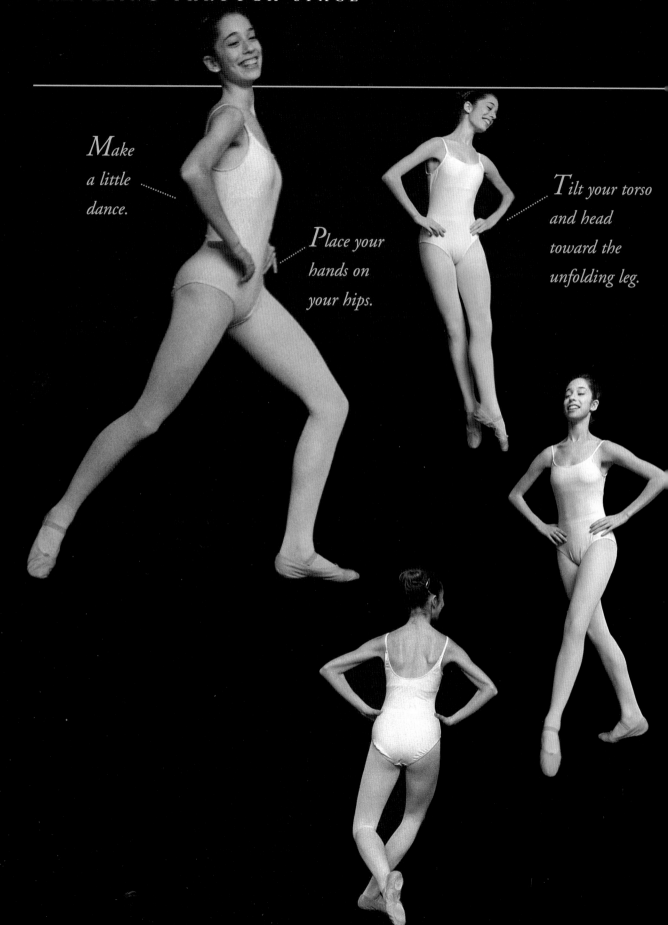

Make a little dance.

Place your hands on your hips.

Tilt your torso and head toward the unfolding leg.

chassé and polka

Chassé (shah-SAY), which means chased or hunted, is both a transfer of weight from one foot to another *and* a traveling step. Here the dancers are using a combination of chassé and skip, which you already know how to do well, to do a kind of polka step in a circle. Start with your right foot front in fifth position. *Développé* (DAY-vloh-PAY—develop or unfold) your right leg to your front, stepping into fourth position plié. Now jump off the floor, quickly closing the back leg to the front leg (chase it!) as you move forward into the air. Land in demi-plié, left foot first, then right. (Your right leg is still in front.) Now bring your left leg front with a low développé. As you pass through, do a little skip on your right foot. Repeat on the left foot.

When you come down from the jump, think "up."

Lift your heels up.

Stretch your feet in the air.

No thuds on the landing!

emboité

E*mboités* (ahm-bwah-TAYZ) are prances that can be small when you want to stay in place or big when you want to travel. Think of emboités as graceful jumps linked together, one after the other, powered by the spring in your legs. This exercise works best when you use both legs efficiently. Start in a strong demi-plié in fifth position. Your body is facing a diagonal, your arms are in third position, and your head is facing front. Push off both feet and land on one foot in a deep demi-plié. Your working leg is lifted high and bent at the knee in *attitude devant* (ah-tih-TYUD dih-VAHN). Now, push off the supporting foot (energy!) and land in a deep demi-plié on the other foot. Jump again, changing feet. And again.

Look out over your forward arm.

Lift your torso high.

Straighten both legs in the air.

grand jeté

By now you're ready to fly. A *grand jeté* (grahn zheh-TAY) is a wonderful leap that can travel fast and skim over the ground or sail high through the air (jeté means "thrown"). If you've ever leaped over a puddle, you already know how to do a grand jeté. It is a combination of a grand battement and a super-stretched arabesque that takes place in the air. You need a good push-off from the floor (that means a good plié) before the jeté and a quiet landing after. Listen carefully to the music. If the rhythm and timing of your jeté are right, you'll soar. If not, you'll feel clunky. Start with a run, called a *glissade* (glee-SAHD). The pattern is: Run, run, leap. Run, run, leap. You may want to practice leaping over a big pile of coats.

*Long neck
and back*

*Long,
stretched
arms*

*Elegant arms
and hands*

révérence

Class is finally over. But before you dash off to the dressing room, you perform what is called *révérence* (ray-vay-RAHNS). This exercise is a formal way of saying thank you and good-bye: a bow if you're a boy, a curtsy if you're a girl. Révérence reminds you that as much as you love to move, dancing is also for the pleasure of your audience, whether it's your teacher and pianist, your family, or a theater full of people. Sometimes révérence is quite elaborate, with lots of steps and gestures. The dancers here are performing révérence simply and elegantly.

Ballerinas started dancing on their toes about 200 years ago. The idea was to create the illusion of lightness, of skimming over the floor—think of butterflies and fairies. But creating all that magic is really hard work, and it requires strong bones and muscles. Girls don't start dancing *sur le pointe* (syer leh pwahnt), or on pointe, until they're about eleven or twelve and have been studying for several years. Your teacher will tell you when it's time.

pointe work

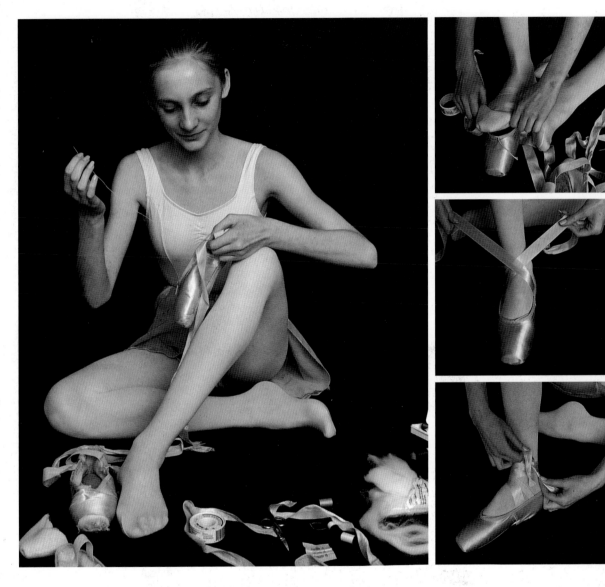

Pointe shoes are molded by hand out of several layers of satin, burlap, paste, and special materials and are hard at the toe. (Like great chefs, pointe shoemakers never give away their secret ingredients.) More or less paste is used, depending on how hard the toe area, or box, needs to be. Some ballets have lots of turns and relevés and dancers might want a stronger, newer box. Other ballets, with many jumps and easier pointe work, might need a softer, older shoe. Here you see all the necessities that go along with pointe work and a couple of the most common exercises. They're similar to the ones you're learning, but Alina is doing them on pointe.

partnering

Sometimes you work with a partner to make a movement happen. This is one reason why all ballet dancers must learn the same language. _Pas-de-deux_ (pah-dih-DYEH), or step for two, is a conversation without words in which you learn to listen and respond to your partner as you would listen and respond to music. Though you won't start practicing pas-de-deux until you've been dancing for several years and are quite strong, you and a partner might have fun trying to help each other balance. Ask a friend or your brother or sister to be your partner. Ask your partner to hold your waist as you stand in passé relevé. Can your partner find your balance? You should not be wiggling all over the place like overcooked spaghetti. You need to keep your body strong and in one piece!

stepping out

By now you're probably wondering where else your first lessons in ballet might take you. How about to a ballet performance? Ask your family to take you to the theater, where you'll experience the thrilling moment when the curtain goes up, and the music, lights, costumes, and dancing come magically together. Notice how the dancers communicate with one another and how their gestures and expressions invite you into the world they're creating onstage. Watch closely, and you'll see how they turn the ballet technique they've worked so hard on in class into an art filled with personality and grace.